Design: Helen Johnson
Recipes: Helen Walsh
Recipe Photography: Peter Barry
Jacket and Illustration Artwork: Jane Winton,
courtesy of Bernard Thornton Artists

CHARTWELL BOOKS
A division of Book Sales, Inc.
POST OFFICE BOX 7100
114 Northfield Avenue
Edison, N.J. 08818-7100

CLB 4577
© 1995 CLB Publishing
Godalming, Surrey, U.K.
All rights reserved
Printed and bound in Singapore
ISBN 0-7858-0293-2

THE LITTLE BOOK
· OF ·

Irish
RECIPES

*The authentic taste of Ireland in a
wholesome collection of tasty recipes*

CHARTWELL
BOOKS, INC.

Introduction

Ireland's great agricultural base and its long-established tradition of warm hospitality have always combined to produce a rich seam of wholesome, uncomplicated fare. In the days of the Brehon Laws – the rules of etiquette laid down in the 5th century which governed how a host must receive guests – the importance of offering good food was not underestimated.

Visitors to the island have always been treated with friendly hospitality – medieval monastic cooks may have lived frugally themselves, but their guests were offered hearty meals of bread and capons, salmon and oysters, all washed down with wine or ale. Earlier still, in the 10th century when Dublin was a Viking city, the Irish menu was amazingly rich and varied. Archeological remains show that beef, pork and mutton were eaten, as well as swans, geese, ravens and, naturally, cockles and mussels. Seeds recovered from rubbish pits indicate that dessert courses included apples, strawberries, cherries, plums and hazelnuts. The Viking presence in Ireland left a valuable culinary legacy. The art of preserving staple foods such as fish and meats by drying, salting, smoking and pickling was an important step forward for the native people.

Today, Ireland boasts an impressive variety of fresh produce from its rivers, coast and lush farmlands. From the excellent heather pastures of Kerry and Wicklow comes tender Irish lamb and beef, while the well-stocked and unpolluted waters yield the freshest of fish and seafood. Potatoes have been a staple part of the Irish diet since their introduction in the 16th century, and their sweet, nutty flavor is unlike anything grown elsewhere. They also have a particular historical significance, as it was the failure of the potato crop in 1845 that led to the devastating famine which forced 2 million Irish to emigrate to the United States.

Of course Irish cooking is also influenced by its unique alcoholic specialties. Stout and whiskey are frequently used to enhance everything from stews to cakes and sweet desserts. Ireland boasts the world's oldest licensed distillery – distilling first began at Bushmills in County Antrim in 1494, and it became a licensed establishment in 1608.

As in other lands, seasonal dishes remain popular in Ireland: a particular favorite at Hallowe'en is Barm Brack, a fruity bread that is traditionally baked with a ring inside it to indicate who among the diners will be the next to be married! Colcannon, a simple yet delicious mix of hot potato, cabbage, butter and milk, seasoned with nutmeg, is also eaten at this time. Spiced Beef, with its lengthy preparation, is popular at Christmas.

This book provides a tempting selection of authentic Irish recipes, from traditional and hearty meats to delicately-flavored fish dishes, which demonstrate the wholesome nature and splendid variety of Irish cooking.

Dublin Bay Prawn Cocktail

SERVES 4

Dublin Bay prawns are expensive and often difficult to find, but shrimp are a good substitute.

PREPARATION: 15 minutes

5-6 lettuce leaves
1 pound cooked, shelled shrimp (frozen shrimp will do)
A little chopped parsley
4 jumbo shrimp
4 lemon wedges for garnish

Cocktail sauce
2 tbsps tomato paste
1 tsp Worcestershire sauce
2 tsps lemon juice
4 tsps medium sherry
4 heaping tbsps mayonnaise
2 tbsps whipped cream

1. To make the sauce, add the tomato paste, Worcestershire sauce, lemon juice and sherry to the mayonnaise and mix well. Fold in the whipped cream.

2. Shred the lettuce finely and divide between four glass goblets.

3. Place equal amounts of shrimp on top of the lettuce. Just before serving, coat the shrimp with the cocktail sauce and sprinkle a pinch of the chopped parsley on top of each.

4. Garnish with a jumbo shrimp and a lemon wedge on each glass. Serve with buttered brown soda bread.

Potato Soup

SERVES 6-8

Potatoes are synonymous with Ireland, and are found in everything from soups to scones and bread.

PREPARATION: 20 minutes
COOKING: 1 hour

---

2 pounds potatoes
2 onions
1 small carrot
¼ cup butter
5 cups light broth
2½ cups milk
Bay leaf, parsley and thyme
Salt and pepper
Cream and chives for garnish

---

1. Peel and slice the potatoes, onions and carrot.

2. Melt butter in a large saucepan and sweat the onions in it until soft but not brown.

3. Add potatoes and carrot. Stir in the stock and milk.

4. Tie the bay leaf, thyme and parsley together and add to the pan, along with pepper and salt to taste.

5. Simmer gently for about an hour then purée in a liquidizer or food processor.

6. Add some cream before serving and sprinkle with chopped chives.

Broiled Trout with Almonds

SERVES 4

This simple recipe brings out all the fresh flavour of trout.

PREPARATION: 10 minutes
COOKING: 15 minutes

---

4 fresh trout, cleaned
1 lemon, quartered
¼ cup butter
¼ cup slivered almonds
Parsley for garnish

---

1. Place a lemon wedge in the cavity of each trout.

2. Line a broiler pan with buttered foil and carefully lay the fish on it. Smear a little butter on each.

3. Preheat the broiler and cook the trout under it for 5 minutes. Turn them very carefully, put a little more butter on top and broil for another 5 minutes.

4. Keep the fish warm on plates while you toss the almonds in the butter in the broiler pan and brown them under the broiler.

5. Sprinkle the browned almonds over the fish. Serve with a garnish of lemon slices and parsley.

Poached Salmon Garni

SERVES 8-10

Ireland's fruitful waters provide an abundance of fresh fish. Salmon is, of course, one of the favorites, and this simple recipe is an excellent way of preparing it.

PREPARATION: 2-3 hours
COOKING: 20-30 minutes

1 fresh salmon, approx 2½ pounds, cleaned, with head removed
1 tbsp vinegar
1 large lettuce
5-6 hard-cooked eggs
1 lemon, sliced
1 cucumber
3-4 firm tomatoes
4 sprigs of fresh dill for garnish
Mayonnaise

1. Cut the fish in half, crosswise. Place each piece on a well-buttered piece of foil and make a package, folding the join several times and folding in the ends.

2. Place the two pieces in a saucepan large enough to hold them side by side, cover them with cold water, add the vinegar, and bring slowly to a boil.

3. Gently turn the packages over in the water. Turn off the heat, cover the pan, and leave to cool.

4. Before the fish is completely cold, put the packages on a large plate, unwrap them and carefully skin and bone the fish.

5. Divide each section into serving-size pieces along the grain of the fish.

6. Lay the salmon portions in two rows, the length of one or two serving platters, with lettuce leaves between them. Slice the hard-cooked eggs and arrange slices overlapping.

7. Allow a slice of lemon for each salmon portion and place accordingly. Slice the cucumber and tomatoes and arrange together on the platter.

8. Garnish the salmon with sprigs of dill and serve with mayonnaise.

Spiced Beef

SERVES 6

*Served cold and thinly sliced, this is a great favorite in most Irish households
at Christmas time.*

PREPARATION: 1 week for marinating
COOKING: 6 hours, plus overnight standing

Flavoring mix
1 tsp powdered mace
6 finely ground cloves
1 tsp crushed black peppercorns
Large clove garlic, minced
1 tsp allspice
2 tbsps molasses
2 heaping tbsps brown sugar
1 pound coarse salt

6-pound piece of fresh brisket, sirloin tip or eye
   of round
1 tsp ground cloves
2 bay leaves
1 onion peeled and quartered
2 carrots, peeled and quartered

1. Blend together all the spices and flavorings
for the mix.

2. Place beef in a large dish and rub well all
over with the mixture.

3. Refrigerate in a covered bowl. Repeat this
process every day for a week, turning the meat
and rubbing in the spices which will now be
mixed with the juices drawn from the meat.

4. Tie the meat up firmly with string and rub in
a final teaspoon of ground cloves.

5. Place in a large, deep pan with the bay
leaves, onion and carrots. Cover with cold
water and bring slowly to a boil. Skim the
surface, then cover the pan and simmer slowly
for about six hours.

6. When cool enough to handle, remove from
the cooking liquid, place in a dish and cover
with a weighted plate for about 8 hours, or
overnight. Slice very thinly and serve.

Irish Stew

SERVES 4

It is important not to use too much liquid in this classic Irish dish. Cooking should be slow so that the dish does not dry out.

PREPARATION: 20 minutes
COOKING: 2½ hours

---

2 pounds boned mutton or 3 pounds rib chops
2 pounds potatoes
2 large onions
Salt and pepper
1 tbsp fresh, chopped thyme and parsley or
   1 tsp dried thyme
1½ cups water
Chopped parsley for garnish

---

1. Trim the meat, leaving a little of the fat on. Peel and slice the potatoes and onions.

2. Season the meat and vegetables with salt, pepper, and herbs. Then, starting and finishing with a layer of potatoes, layer the potatoes, meats and onions in a large casserole or baking dish.

3. Add the water and cover tightly. Either simmer on a very low heat on the top of the stove for 2½ hours or cook in a 275°F oven for the same length of time.

4. The pot or casserole should be shaken occasionally to prevent the potatoes from sticking and you should check that the liquid has not dried out. The finished stew should not be too runny as the potatoes should thicken it sufficiently.

5. Brown the top potato layer under a hot broiler and serve sprinkled with chopped parsley.

Crubeens

SERVES 4

This humble dish was once ubiquitous in Ireland's late-night bars, and although less common today, it remains a delicious and satisfying snack.

PREPARATION: 5 minutes
COOKING: 3 hours

4 pig's feet
1 onion, quartered
2 carrots, quartered
½ tsp salt
Few peppercorns
2 bay leaves
Sprigs of fresh parsley and thyme
Lettuce and tomato for garnish

1. Put the pig's feet, onion, carrots, salt, peppercorns, and the herbs in a large pan.

2. Cover with cold water, bring to a boil and simmer for 3 hours.

3. Serve the pig's feet surrounded by lettuce and with a tomato garnish.

Beef Braised in Guinness

SERVES 4

This delicious combination produces a hearty stew perfect for a cold winter's evening.

PREPARATION: 15 minutes
COOKING: 1 hour 45 minutes

1½ pounds chuck or round roast, about
   1 inch thick
2 medium onions
½ pound carrots
2 heaping tbsps all-purpose flour
Salt and pepper
2-3 tbsps cooking oil
½ tsp fresh basil, minced
⅔ cup Guinness
1 tsp honey
⅔ cup beef broth or water

---

1. Cut the meat into about twelve pieces.

2. Peel the onions and chop them into fairly small dice. Peel the carrots and slice them into sticks.

3. Place the flour in a flat dish and mix in 1 tsp of salt and a good sprinkling of pepper.

4. Heat the oil in a sauté pan, add the onions and cook until soft. Transfer them with a slotted spoon to a large, shallow, greased ovenproof dish.

5. Dip the pieces of meat in the seasoned flour and brown them in the fat in the pan. Remove these as they are cooked and place in the dish on top of the onions, in a single layer. Arrange the carrots around them. If necessary, add a little more oil to the pan and stir in the remainder of the seasoned flour.

6. Cook for a minute or two, stirring constantly, then add the basil and the Guinness. Allow to boil for a minute or two, then add the honey and the stock. Return to a boil and pour over the meat. Cover the dish either with a lid or with foil and cook in the oven at 325°F for 1½ hours.

7. If the gravy looks as though it needs thickening, mix 1 tsp of arrowroot with 2 tbsps of cold water and stir into the gravy 15 minutes before the end of cooking time.

Boiled Chicken and Parsley Sauce

SERVES 4-6

Cabbage and lovely floury potatoes boiled in their jackets are an ideal accompaniment to this traditional dish.

PREPARATION: 15 minutes
COOKING: 2½-3 hours

2-3 ounces chicken fat
1 large boiling fowl weighing about 5-6 pounds
Salt and pepper
1 onion, chopped
1 carrot, chopped
1 turnip, chopped
1 stick celery, chopped
A bouquet garni

Parsley sauce
¼ cup butter
½ cup all-purpose flour
1¼ cups broth, reserved from cooking the chicken
1¼ cups milk
Cupful of chopped parsley
Salt and pepper

1. Melt the chicken fat in a large, deep saucepan. Wash and dry the bird, inside and out, and season well with salt and pepper.

2. Slightly brown the fowl in the fat, then remove from the pan, and add the vegetables. Turn them in the fat for a few minutes then add the chicken and cover with cold water.

3. Add salt, pepper and bouquet garni. Bring slowly to a boil, skim, then cover the pan and simmer slowly for 2½-3 hours, until tender when pierced in the thickest part of the leg. When the bird is cooked, remove it from the pan and keep hot on a serving dish.

4. Melt the butter in a saucepan, stir in the flour and cook for 1 minute. Remove from heat and gradually stir in 1¼ cups of the strained chicken broth.

5. Return to the heat and, when the mixture has thickened, gradually add the milk, and continue cooking until it boils again.

6. Lower the heat and cook for a further 2 minutes; add parsley and season with salt and pepper. Pour the sauce into a gravy boat or jug and serve with the chicken.

Stuffed Breast of Lamb

SERVES 4

Simply prepared, and enhanced with herbs, this recipe is perfect for this popular cut of meat.

PREPARATION: 30 minutes
COOKING: 1 hour

2-pound breast of lamb, with bones and trimmings reserved
1 medium onion
Salt and pepper
4 cups white bread crumbs
¼ cup chopped lard or butter
½ tsp marjoram
½ tsp thyme
Grated rind of ½ lemon
1 egg
1 tbsp all-purpose flour

1. Place the lamb bones in a saucepan with half the onion and some salt and pepper. Cover with water, bring to a boil, skim, and simmer for half an hour, covered.

2. Mix the bread crumbs, lard or butter, herbs, lemon rind, a little salt and pepper and the other half of the onion, minced, and bind with the egg. Add 2-3 tbsps of the bone stock and spread the stuffing on the breast of lamb.

3. Roll up, starting at the wide end. Tie up firmly with string and place in a greased roasting pan. Bake in a 400°F oven for 1 hour. Transfer the meat to a serving dish and keep hot while you make the gravy.

4. Drain off any excess fat from the roasting pan, retaining about two tablespoons. Stir in the flour, and heat on the stove until mixture browns. Stir in about a cupful of the stock. Bring to a boil, stirring constantly. Boil for a few minutes and then strain into a gravy boat and serve with the stuffed lamb.

Colcannon

SERVES 4

*Colcannon is a traditional potato and cabbage dish closely associated with Halloween.
It is an excellent accompaniment for boiled ham.*

PREPARATION: 10 minutes
COOKING: 20 minutes

½ cup finely chopped onion, leek, green onion
  or scallion
¼ cup butter
¼ cup milk
1 pound cooked mashed potatoes
1½ cups cooked cabbage

---

1. Melt the butter in a large skillet. Add the onion and fry gently until softened.

2. Add the milk and the well-mashed potatoes, and stir until heated through.

3. Mince the cabbage finely and beat into the mixture over a low heat until the mixture is pale green and fluffy.

Boxty Pancakes

SERVES 6

These unusual pancakes are made with a mixture of cooked and raw potatoes combined with fat, flour and milk.

PREPARATION: 20 minutes
COOKING: 15 minutes

½ pound raw potatoes
½ pound cooked, mashed potatoes
1 tsp salt
1 tsp baking soda
2 cups all-purpose flour
Pepper
¼ cup butter, margarine or bacon drippings
Milk

---

1. Peel and grate the raw potatoes. Wrap them tightly in a cloth and squeeze over a bowl to extract as much of the starch liquid as possible.

2. Thoroughly blend the grated raw potato into the cooked, mashed potato.

3. Pour the liquid off the bowl of potato starch and scrape the starch into the potato mixture.

4. Sift the salt and baking soda with the flour and add to the potatoes; mix well. Add the melted fat and mix again. Add as much milk as necessary to make the mixture into a batter of dropping consistency, and season with pepper.

5. Cook in spoonfuls on a greased skillet until crispy and golden on both sides.

 31

Potato Cakes

SERVES 8

For the best results, use old floury potatoes.

PREPARATION: 20 minutes
COOKING: 8-12 minutes

---

1 cup all-purpose flour
½ tsp salt
½ tsp baking powder
2 tbsps butter
2¾ cups mashed potato
Bacon drippings or melted butter

---

1. Sift flour, salt and baking powder into a mixing bowl. Rub in the butter.

2. Mix in the potatoes and knead into a ball.

3. Cut this dough in half and roll out each piece into a ½-inch-thick circle on a floured board or work surface.

4. Divide each cake into 4 segments.

5. Grease a skillet with some bacon drippings or melted butter and heat well.

6. Add the wedges of potato cake and cook them for 2-3 minutes on each side.

Apple Cake

This simple, inexpensive recipe makes good use of store cupboard ingredients.

PREPARATION: 20 minutes
COOKING: 45 minutes

1 tsp cinnamon
1½ cups self-rising flour
¾ cup butter or margarine
¾ cup superfine sugar
3 eggs
2 tbsps milk
2-3 eating apples, peeled, cored and thinly
  sliced

1. Add the cinnamon to the flour and sift into a bowl.

2. Cream butter and sugar until light and soft.

Beat in 1 egg then add 1 tbsp of the flour and beat in another egg.

3. Repeat this once more then fold in ⅔ of the remaining flour.

4. Stir in the milk then fold in the last of the flour.

5. Grease either a lasagne dish or a roasting pan (about 11 × 8½ inches).

6. Spread half the batter in the bottom, distribute the apple slices over it and cover with the rest of the batter.

7. Bake in a 350°F oven for 15 minutes, then reduce heat to 325°F. Continue baking for 30 minutes until golden brown and firm to the touch.

Summer Pudding

SERVES 8

Raspberries are a great favorite in Ireland and this wonderful old recipe is a good way of using up a glut of fruit.

PREPARATION: 30 minutes, plus overnight
   chilling
COOKING: 5 minutes

Unsliced loaf of white bread
1½ pounds fruit (raspberries, redcurrants and
   blackberries)
½ cup sugar

---

1. First line a pudding bowl with the bread. Cut some slices of bread about ½ inch thick. From one of these cut a round to fit in the bottom of the bowl. For the sides cut the bread in finger pieces, the height of the bowl in length, and, in width, about 1½ inches at one end and 1 inch at the other. Pack these tightly around the sides of the bowl.

2. Gently heat the fruit in a saucepan, adding sugar to taste, until the juice starts to run. While hot, pour into the lined bowl and cover the top with bread.

3. Set it on a plate so as to catch any juice that may flow over.

4. Place a small weighted plate on top. Leave to stand overnight in the refrigerator.

5. When cold, turn out and pour round it any juice that may have run into the plate. Serve with custard, cream or milk.

Barm Brack

MAKES 2 loaves
This fruity bread is traditionally eaten in Ireland at Halloween.

PREPARATION: Preparation and rising time:
  2-3 hours
COOKING: 1 hour 10 minutes

½ tsp salt
½ tsp cinnamon
Pinch grated nutmeg
4 cups all-purpose flour
¼ cup softened butter
⅓ cup superfine sugar
1 cup milk, at room temperature
1 package active dry yeast
1 egg
1¼ cups golden raisins
1 cup currants
½ cup cut mixed peel, chopped

1. Add the salt and spices to the flour and sift into a large mixing bowl. Rub in the butter.

2. Add 1 tsp of the sugar and 1 tsp of the milk to the yeast and mix well.

3. Add the remainder of the sugar to the flour mixture and mix in.

4. Lightly beat the egg, add the milk, and pour this into the yeast mixture.

5. Add this to the flour and beat very well by hand, or in a mixer fitted with a dough hook, until the batter becomes stiff and elastic.

6. Fold in the mixed fruit and cover the bowl with lightly greased plastic wrap. Leave the bowl in a warm place for 1-2 hours, to allow the dough to rise.

7. Divide the mixture between two greased 8½x4½-inch loaf pans, or two 7-inch cake pans. Cover again and allow to rise for 30 minutes.

8. Bake for 1 hour at 375°F in the center of a preheated oven.

9. Dissolve 1 tbsp of sugar in a quarter cup of hot water and brush over brack, return it to the oven for 5 minutes with the heat turned off.

10. Turn out onto a wire rack to cool. Slice and butter.

Irish Soda Bread

MAKES 1 loaf

This popular bread can be bought almost anywhere in Ireland, but is also very easy to make at home.

PREPARATION: 15 minutes
COOKING: 40-45 minutes

---

1 tsp salt
1 tsp sugar
1 heaping tsp cream of tartar
1 heaping tsp baking soda
2 cups all-purpose flour
4 cups whole-wheat flour
2 cups sour milk or fresh milk mixed with
   1 tbsp yogurt

---

1. Add the salt, sugar, cream of tartar and baking soda to the all-purpose flour. Sift into a large mixing bowl.

2. Add whole-wheat flour and mix thoroughly with a round-ended knife, using a lifting motion to aerate the mixture.

3. Make a well in the center and add milk, mixing until the dough leaves the sides of the bowl clean.

4. Knead into a ball, flatten slightly and place on a greased cookie tray. Cut a cross into the top of the loaf.

5. Brush the top with a little milk, and bake in a preheated oven at 400°F for 40 minutes.

6. Remove from the oven, turn loaf upside down and return to the oven for a further 5 minutes. The loaf is done when it sounds hollow when tapped on the base.

7. Wrap the bread in a slightly dampened cloth and stand on its side to cool. Cut into quarters, slice and butter generously.

Yellow Man

YIELDS about 2 pounds

This confection has been associated for centuries with the "Ould Lammas Fair," which takes place every year at Ballycastle, County Antrim.

PREPARATION: 15 minutes plus setting time
COOKING: 45 minutes

---

1 heaping tbsp butter
1 cup brown sugar
4 cups corn syrup
2 tbsps distilled white vinegar
1 tsp baking powder

---

1. Melt the butter in a saucepan and coat the inside of the pan with it. Add the sugar, syrup, and the vinegar. Stir over a low heat until the sugar and syrup have melted.

2. Bring the mixture to a boil and cook without stirring until the temperature reaches 290°F on a sugar thermometer, or a little of the mixture sets when dropped into a cup of cold water.

4. Add the baking powder, which will make the mixture foam up. Stir well again, and allow the bubbles to subside then pour into a greased pan and leave until almost set before cutting into squares. It may also be turned out onto a slab after the boiling process, then pulled until it becomes pale yellow in color.

5. When it hardens it can be broken into pieces with a little hammer.

Index

Beef Braised in Guinness